Animal Teams

Orca Pods

by Trudy Becker

FOCUS READERS

BEACON

www.focusreaders.com

Focus Readers is distributed by North Star Editions:
sales@northstareditions.com | 888-417-0195

Produced for Focus Readers by Red Line Editorial.

Photographs ©: Shutterstock Images, cover, 1, 4, 6, 8, 12, 16, 19, 22, 26, 29; iStockphoto, 10, 14–15, 20; Robert Hernandez/Science Source, 25

Library of Congress Cataloging-in-Publication Data
Names: Becker, Trudy, author.
Title: Orca pods / by Trudy Becker.
Description: Mendota Heights, MN: Focus Readers, [2025] | Series: Animal teams | Includes index. | Audience: Grades 2-3
Identifiers: LCCN 2023050718 (print) | LCCN 2023050719 (ebook) | ISBN 9798889981923 (hardcover) | ISBN 9798889982487 (paperback) | ISBN 9798889983576 (pdf) | ISBN 9798889983040 (ebook)
Subjects: LCSH: Killer whale--Juvenile literature. | Killer whale--Behavior--Juvenile literature. | Familial behavior in animals--Juvenile literature.
Classification: LCC QL737.C432 B435 2025 (print) | LCC QL737.C432 (ebook) | DDC 599.53/6--dc23/eng/20231130
LC record available at https://lccn.loc.gov/2023050718
LC ebook record available at https://lccn.loc.gov/2023050719

Printed in the United States of America
Mankato, MN
082024

About the Author

Trudy Becker lives in Minneapolis, Minnesota. She likes exploring new places and loves anything involving books.

Table of Contents

CHAPTER 1

On the Hunt 5

CHAPTER 2

Raising Families 9

THAT'S AMAZING!

Playtime 14

CHAPTER 3

Sharing Information 17

CHAPTER 4

Hunting 23

Focus on Orca Pods • 28

Glossary • 30

To Learn More • 31

Index • 32

Chapter 1

On the Hunt

A group of orcas swim through the ocean. They are on the hunt. Soon, the orcas find a pack of gray whales. Many of the whales are big and strong. But one looks smaller. It is weak.

Orcas can swim more than 30 miles per hour (48 km/h) at full speed.

Orcas can travel more than 40 miles (64 km) a day to find food.

The orcas rush toward the weak whale. They work together to separate it from the group. Then the orcas attack. They take turns ramming the whale. Some orcas bite it, too. They pull on the whale's fins and flip it over.

The whale struggles. But the orcas keep going. They don't let the whale's blowhole reach the surface. Finally, the whale drowns. The orcas have won their meal.

Did You Know?

Orcas are also called killer whales.

Chapter 2

Raising Families

Orcas live and work together in **social** groups. The groups are called pods. Some pods are small. They have just a few orcas. Other pods are larger. They can have up to 40 orcas.

Orcas usually swim close to the surface of the water.

A mother orca gives birth to one calf at a time.

Orca pods are **matrilineal**. They are led by females. Each pod has at least one mother and her calves. Resident orcas are one type of orca. They stay with their mothers their whole lives. Their pods can have up to four generations. Transient orcas are different. Daughters might leave when they have their own calves. So, their pods are smaller. They often have just one mother and her calves.

Orca pods do many activities together. For example, the whole pod helps teach young orcas. Pod members also care for one another. They help the young, sick, and injured. Some younger mothers focus mostly on their own calves.

Orcas jump for many reasons. They might do it to communicate or to look for other pod members.

The oldest females look out for the whole pod. They are more likely to share food with the group.

Working as a team helps the pod succeed. Young orcas learn the pod's **culture**. First, they watch other orcas. Then they copy what they see. In that way, calves figure out how to behave. They discover what to eat. They learn how to hunt. And they learn how to communicate with other orcas. They can grow up to help the pod thrive.

Did You Know?

Most social animals have big brains. Orcas have some of the biggest brains of all ocean animals.

THAT'S AMAZING!

Playtime

Orca pods don't just work together. They also play together. When orcas play, they often **breach** the water. They belly flop with big splashes. They smack their tails down on the water, too. Sometimes groups play for hours. It is part of their social connection. Orcas can strengthen their bonds.

When playing, orcas sometimes touch boats. They might bump into the boats. Sometimes they even break parts of boats. This behavior can scare people. But orcas rarely attack humans.

In the summer of 2023, orcas interacted with boats more often than normal.

Chapter 3

Sharing Information

Pods have many ways to share information. They make sounds such as clicks, whistles, and pulsed calls. Some orcas make loud chattering noises, too.

Orcas use whistles and calls to communicate. Clicks are used for echolocation.

Orcas also use **echolocation**. Their sounds bounce off things and come back. That helps orcas find out what is around them. They learn sizes, shapes, and distances. Then orcas can pass that information to others in their pod.

These forms of communication are useful. Orcas can share where to go next. They can signal if danger is near. They can all act together.

But different pods communciate in different ways. That's because

Orcas can use body language as another form of communication.

each pod has a unique **dialect**. The length, pitch, and pattern of their sounds are different. Before birth, a baby orca hears its mother's sounds. It learns and remembers.

Orca sounds can travel 10 miles (16 km) underwater.

Later, the baby copies others in the pod. That is how a pod's dialect gets passed down. The dialect stays the same across generations.

Orcas can also communicate between pods. Certain shared calls make that possible. Different pods across the same **clan** use those calls. Sometimes pods without similar dialects communicate, too. They don't use similar calls. But they might play or hunt together. When these types of pods interact, they are called a community.

Did You Know?

Some orcas can copy sounds of other ocean animals. For example, they can imitate calls of bottlenose dolphins.

Chapter 4

Hunting

Orcas are one of the top **predators** in the ocean. Their prey depends on the pod's culture and **habitat**. For instance, transient orcas eat seals, sea lions, and porpoises.

An adult orca's teeth are about 3 inches (7.6 cm) long.

Residents mostly eat salmon. Offshore orcas mostly eat sharks.

As with everything they do, orcas also hunt together. They use different strategies for different prey. One tactic is making big waves. Orcas do this to catch seals on ice. The orcas rush forward quickly. Then they slip under the ice. Strong waves knock the seals into the water.

Some orcas hunt by **herding**. They swim fast and herd schools of

Sometimes orcas might trap seals on the ice. They chip away at the ice to make it smaller.

fish into one area. Then they hit the fish with their tails. Orcas can also beach themselves. That means the orcas go up on the sand. They catch sea lions or elephant seals there. Then they ride the waves back out.

Resident orcas may travel long distances to find salmon.

Or they might flop or hop back into the water.

Orcas can even hit prey such as sharks. This move is almost like a karate chop. First, an orca turns a shark onto its back. That makes the shark stay still. Then the orca smacks the shark with its fin.

After catching prey, orcas share their food. The calves might not have helped hunt. But they watched and learned. When they are older, they will help. That way, the pod can continue catching food.

Did You Know?

An adult orca eats approximately 500 pounds (227 kg) of food a day.

FOCUS ON

Orca Pods

Write your answers on a separate piece of paper.

1. Write a few sentences explaining some ways that orca pods hunt.
2. If you were an orca, would you want to live in a big pod or a small pod? Why?
3. What kind of orca eats mostly salmon?
   - A. resident orca
   - B. transient orca
   - C. offshore orca
4. Why might orcas not help with hunting when they are young?
   - A. Young orcas move too quickly to hunt with the group.
   - B. Young orcas have not learned hunting skills yet.
   - C. Young orcas do not like helping the group.

5. What does **unique** mean in this book?

*That's because each pod has a **unique** dialect. The length, pitch, and pattern of their sounds are different.*

A. the same
B. not like any other
C. very big

6. What does **thrive** mean in this book?

*They learn how to hunt. And they learn how to communicate with other orcas. They can grow up to help the pod **thrive**.*

A. do well
B. struggle
C. hide

Answer key on page 32.

Glossary

breach
To leap out of the water.

clan
A group of orca pods that share similar forms of communication.

culture
A set of behaviors that animals learn from one another.

dialect
A set of calls that one group of social animals uses together.

echolocation
A way of bouncing sound off objects to figure out how close they are.

habitat
The type of place where plants or animals normally grow or live.

herding
Making animals move as a group into one area.

matrilineal
When family relationships are traced through females.

predators
Animals that hunt other animals for food.

social
Likely to spend time with other animals of the same type.

To Learn More

BOOKS

Adamson, Thomas K. *Great White Shark vs. Killer Whale*. Minneapolis: Bellwether Media, 2020.

Amin, Anita Nahta. *Is It a Dolphin or a Porpoise?* North Mankato, MN: Capstone Press, 2022.

Jaycox, Jaclyn. *Orca Cows: Leaders of the Pod*. North Mankato, MN: Capstone Press, 2023.

NOTE TO EDUCATORS

Visit **www.focusreaders.com** to find lesson plans, activities, links, and other resources related to this title.

Index

B
breaching, 14

C
calves, 10–11, 13, 20, 27
clan, 21
communication, 13, 17–21

D
dialect, 19–21

E
echolocation, 18

G
gray whales, 5

H
herding, 24–25
hunting, 5–7, 13, 21, 23–27

O
offshore orcas, 24

P
playing, 14
predators, 23
prey, 6–7, 23–27

R
resident orcas, 10, 24

T
transient orcas, 11, 23

Answer Key: 1. Answers will vary; **2.** Answers will vary; **3.** A; **4.** B; **5.** B; **6.** A